Ult

Will Writing

How to create your own Will

Written & presented by

Vivek Kumar Bajaj

References:

The CFP$_{CM}$ study material of Financial Planning Academy & Mandar Learning Academy

This book is dedicated to my beautiful wife and my little Angel.

About the Author...

Vivek Kumar Bajaj is a Mutual fund distributor, insurance consultant and Income tax return advisor.

Vivek is working in the financial sector since 2002. He started his career as an insurance advisor with ICICI prudential life insurance. In these last 18 years, he works with a single motto "Long term relationship with customers". Currently, he is working as a channel partner with prudent corporate advisory services.

He is passionate about spreading knowledge, which he accumulated in these 18 years. He works seven days a week for the betterment and profitability of his clients.

Beyond helping clients manage their investments, he likes spending time in nature and mountains. He loves safari and car drive in forest areas.

Creating wills and estate plans essentially refer to choosing heirs and appointing guardians.

Posted by: Chicago Estate Planning Lawyer in legallistings.us

CONTENTS

INTRODUCTION

Every individual ignores will writing. We think earning is the only goal of our life. We put everything in creating estates and one day journey ends, leaving all the estates to court. The financial protection of our loved ones is on the stack because of our ignorance.

Sometimes we ignore appointing a legal heir because it's a very complicated legal process. In Indian law and by every country's laws, the Will writing process is kept as simple as ordering food online. You do not need to be an expert for your Will writing.

Will is your last wish list. Law always binds according to your Will, if you have a legally valid Will. Your all estates inherit as per your Will. By creating a Will, you instruct your estate's transfer to your beneficiary and as per your wish.

In this book, you will learn *"how to create your Will by yourself"*. No need for any legal person or law expert. This book will guide you step by step to create your legally valid Will and answers all the questions in your mind.

This book focuses on and encouraging individuals to write their Will for the financial protection of their loved ones.

Have a safe and sound future!

Vivek Kumar Bajaj

Author, IFA & Consultant

CHAPTER ONE

WHAT IS WILL?

"A will is the legal declaration of the intention of the testator, with respect to his property which he desires to be carried into effect after his death."

-Definition by Indian Succession Act, 1925

A will is a legal document where a person writes down his/her wishes and instructions relating to his/her wealth and appoint a guardian to his/her minor children. A will ensures that a testator's wishes regarding his estate will be fulfilled after his/her death.

WHO CAN WRITE A WILL?

Any person can create a will. For a valid will, the testator must be in sound mental health without undue influence and must be above 18 years of age. A Will can be prepared any time during the lifetime of a testator. Will can be change any time during the life of a testator. Will can be change any number of times; there is no restriction on changes. The last will stands as a valid will. If a person dies without any Will, his/her estate's disposal is done according to law.

CAN I WRITE MY WILL?

Yes, you can write your Will by yourself, after all, it's your final wishes. Different jurisdiction has different laws, but one point is standard, all laws encourage the Will writer to pen their last wishes by yourself.

There is no impact on the legality of Will, whether it is handwritten or computerized. Law is very liberal and more or less supports your convenience to make sure you write your Will. Laws don't care about how you write a Will. You can even write your Will on a tissue paper which is highly not recommendable. Just write your will in your language and must be clear to read and understand.

DO WILL NEED A FIXED FORMAT?

There is no fixed format for a Will. You can write as per your choice and convenience. The Will must be signed and dated. The date of a Will must be the day you signed the Will. You can use any standard format available online or illustrate in this book later.

CHARACTERISTICS OF A VALID WILL

A legally valid will must have the following characteristics:

1. **Legal declaration:** The documents purporting to be a Will must be legally valid. All documents must be prepared as per the law and

must be executed by the legally competent person. The will must be the testator's voluntary act.

2. **Testator's death:** The Will must be effective only after the death of a testator. If the document has provisions intended to affect the testator in his lifetime, it is not a valid Will.

3. **Disposition of estate:** The documents must be relating to the disposal of an estate of the testator. If there is no estate involved in the declaration, it is not a valid Will.

4. **Revocability:** Section 62 of the Indian Succession Act provides

that a Will is liable to be revoked or altered by its maker at any time when they are competent to dispose of their property by Will. If any clause stops the maker to alter or revoked, it's not a valid Will.

ATTESTATION AND REGISTRATION OF A WILL

A Will must be signed by the testator in front of two or more witnesses and must be attested by all witnesses. In the event of the death of any witness in the lifetime of the testator, a new Will with new witnesses must be prepared. Beneficiaries under the Will cannot become the witness; otherwise, the bequest in their favour would become invalid.

Registration of a Will is optional, but if registered, it is placed in the registrar's safe custody and therefore cannot be tempered and lost. The non-registration of Will has no impact on the genuineness of the Will. In the case of registered Will, all changes and revisions must be submitted in the registrar office and should also be registered.

EXECUTION OF A WILL

While preparing or writing a Will, the testator must appoint the executor. After the death of the testator, all properties are held by the executor in trust to beneficiaries. The testator can nominate more than one executor. In case of a primary executor's death, the secondary executor will take charge and so on. There is no restriction on the number of executors. In the case of a Will without executor, the court will appoint the executor.

STRUCTURE AND DRAFTING OF A WILL

While drafting a Will, you can start your will with the simple statement: "I, hereby make the will" or "this is the will of ….".

Then appoint the executor and its alternate with the executor's full details and their pay or compensation (if any).

Provide the details of the guardian if you have minor children.

Than simply states your directions for your estate and details of your debt (if any), then provide the details of your debt coverage or how to settle your debt.

In the next para provide your wishes with the exact names of the beneficiaries and what they get.

The Will ends with the signature of the testator and witnesses.

The testator must initial the Will at the end of every page and next to every correction or alteration. Will can be written in any language which is convenient to the testator. Will must be in simple words and clearly convey the message of the testator. The testator can sign or affix their mark to the Will.

Some other points also keep in mind while drafting a Will.

1. A paragraph stating that the person writing the Will is of sound mind and knows that the current document is to be his/her last Will and testament.
2. That the person writing the Will is not under any undue influence (emotionally and intoxicated) and writing in his/her free agency.
3. A statement that clearly mentions that the executor first clears the person's debts and taxes (if any).
4. If there is any specific wish of the testator, mention it.

HOW TO REGISTER WILL?

You can register your Will with the registrar by paying a nominal fee. Physical presence at the registrar's office of the testator and the witnesses is mandatory. However, some persons are exempted from the physical presence at the registrar's office.

1. Any senior citizen unable for a physical presence
2. Any person having infirmity of body
3. Persons in jail
4. Muslim women

In these cases, the registrar can be legally requested for a home or hospital visit.

Stamp paper is not mandatory for the Will or codicil.

As per the Law, only the testator or his/her representative can claim the copy of the Will. After the death of the testator, anyone can apply for the certified copy of the Will. The registrar will give a copy, on producing the death certificate of the testator.

WHAT ELSE YOU CAN INCLUDE IN A WILL.

Transferring your property to your loved ones is not the only thing you can do with your Will. You can also add some points to your Will.

1. **Your last wish for your funeral:** You can also provide details or instructions for your funeral. Sometimes funeral expenses are heavy for the family you left behind. To ease their burden, you can put some money or provide a portion of your estate for your funeral expenses.

2. **Create a trust:** You can also establish a trust through your Will for the beneficiary. Having trust is like a cherry on the top of a cake. You can safeguard the benefits of a minor heir by creating trust and appointing a trustee.

3. **Providing substitute:** You can also provide a replacement for your legal heirs, in the case of an incapacitated heir who will get the share. You can arrange the substitute or appoint the trustee for the incapacitated heir.

4. **Disinheritance:** Where the law provides the facility of transferring the estate to legal heir, it also

gives the testator a right to disinheriting individuals from the estate's share. But it would be best if you always were careful about disinheritance, especially about your children. Sometimes due to emotions we carried out but not realized that denying them is not the solution for family conflicts. You must have proper grounds for disinheritance; otherwise, that section stands invalid. You cannot deny the share of your children in ancestral property.

5. **Your digital identity:** In today's world every person have some digital identity, i.e. email accounts, Google account, social networking accounts, cloud spaces, etc. you

can also include instructions and heir for these accounts.

6. **Your devices:** you can also include short notes related to the password of your laptop, desktop, mobile, etc. Don't write passwords in your will but leave hints or instructions.

UPDATING YOUR WILL

Creating a Will is not the one time process. You have to update the Will whenever there is a change in family or estate. For updating, you just need an annexure to your Will which indicates the changes in the Will. The annexure is also signed with date and place. Two witness signature is again mandatory. This annexure will become part of your Will.

You can also update your Will if you want to add some new wishes or change your existing wishes.

If there are some significant changes, you must write a new Will. The qualification and requirements will be the same when you are writing a new Will.

NOMINATION VERSES LEGAL HEIR

Nobody knows when the journey of life is going to end. In this journey, we take many financial decisions. We invest in many products for our loved ones like bank fixed deposit, insurance, mutual funds, shares, etc. But the question is "what will happen to all investments after the demise of an investor?

Death is inevitable, and nobody can change it. But you can ensure the financial protection of your loved ones. The next question is, how. Most of the persons answer this question as "using the nomination facility". What if, your nominee is not a legal heir? Let's understand the rules of nomination in different products.

1. **Life Insurance:** As per the Insurance Laws (Amendment) Act

2015, the concept of *Beneficial Nominee* has been introduced. Suppose the policy nominee is an immediate family member such as spouse/parents/children. In that case, the death benefit will be paid to the nominee, and another legal heir has no right to claim that amount.

2. **Bank fixed deposit, mutual funds, etc.**: In these products nominee is just a caretaker. He can collect the money from a respective institution and distribute that to the legal heir. The legal heir has full rights to claim this money.

Transferring your estate smoothly as per your wish is more important than anything else. As we know the law gives more importance to the legal heir than the nominee, so just appointing a nominee to your estate is not enough. By drafting a Will, You can ensure your loved ones' financial protection and transfer of your estate according to your wish.

HOW TO EXECUTE THE WILL?

Execution of a Will starts with a Probate. In India, you can obtain probate from the court. Probate is a legal certification issued by the court, and it declares the genuineness of the Will. After you get the probate, the executor will start the disposing of the testator's estates as per the Will.

IMPORTANT POINTS TO BE REMEMBER

1. Your Will must have your identity details like your name, father's and mother's name, your date of birth, place of birth and your current address.

2. The date of preparing your Will must be written in your Will.

3. Executors details must be written in your Will, i.e. name of the

executor, age, relationship with testator and address.

4. Your will must contain the list of immovable property with the address.

5. Your signature with a witness must be in the Will. Without your signature and witnesses, the Will is void.

CHAPTER TWO

SIMPLE FORMATS OF WILL

EXAMPLE FORMAT 1

WILL OF SHRI…….., S/O or D/O SHRI………..

I, Shri/Smt ……………………
son/daughter/wife of Shri ………………,

resident of ...., by religion.............., do hereby revoke all my previous Wills (or) Codicils and declare that this is my last Will, which I make on this ....*(Date)*..................... My Date of Birth is.............

I declare that I am in good health and possess a sound mind. I make this Will without any persuasion or coercion and out of my own independent decision only.

I appoint Shri.......................
Son/daughter of ...., resident of .... to be the executor of this Will. In the even Shri............... were to predecease me, then Shri................, will be the executor of this Will.

I bequeath the following assets to my Husband/Wife, Shri/Smt.................

1. My house located at ....(address).........
2. The bank balance of my savings accounts no......................with ....(bank name & bank address).........
3. My Bank fixed deposits in ....(bank name).....bearing ....(FD receipt nos)........
4. The proceeds of my Term insurance policy ....(Policy no)......, from.......(insurance company name).........
5. The contents of bank locker no........., with bank............, bank address..............

I bequeath the following assets to my son/daughter Shri/Smt..............

1. Residential Plot no........, located at................
2. My car with registration no..........
3. *My mutual fund investments with folio numbers....................... (Attached annexure with the list of folios)*
4. Any other asset not mentioned in this Will but of which I am the owner.

I own all the above assets. No one else has rights on these properties.

Signature/Thumb impression of Testator

(Full name....)

Date:

Place:

Witnesses

We hereby attest that this Will has been signed by Shri.............as his last Will at ....(Place)......... in the joint presence of himself and us. The testator is in sound mind and made this Will without any coercion.

Signature of Witness (1)

 (Name &
Address)

Signature of Witness (2)

(Name & Address)

EXAMPLE FORMAT 2

LAST WILL AND TESTAMENT OF

_____(your name)_____

_____(Date)_____

I, _____(your
name)_____,
son/daughter of
_____ residing at
_____(address)_____
being of sound mind, in a good healthy
condition and without any undue favor,
declare this to be my Last Will and
Testament. I revoke all wills and codicils
previously made by me.

I appoint _____ as primary executor to administer this Will, and ask that he/she be permitted to serve without Court supervision. If _____ is unwilling or unable to serve, then I appoint _____ to serve as my primary executor and ask that he/she be permitted to serve without Court supervision and without posting bond.

I direct my primary executor to pay out of my residuary estate all of the expenses of my last illness, administration expenses, all legally enforceable creditor claims, all central, state and local taxes and charges imposed because of my death without seeking reimbursement from or charging any person for any part of the taxes and charges paid, and if necessary, reasonable funeral expenses without the necessity of an order of the court approving said expenses.

I bequeath, and give my _____*(details of property or bank or anything in possession)*_____

_____

to _____(name of beneficiary)_____ ____.

(Add for all assets and all beneficiaries)

Signature/Thumb impression of Testator

(Full name....)

Date:

Place:

SELF-PROVING AFFIDAVIT

This document, consisting of this and annexures *(mention number of pages)* was signed and acknowledged by Testator as his/her Last Will and Testament in our presence, and we, at his/her request, and in his/her presence, and the presence of each other, have subscribed our names as witnesses.

Signature of Witness (1)

 (Name &
Address)

Signature of Witness (2)

(Name & Address)

CHAPTER THREE

LAWS RELATING TO WILL

There are three types of succession acts in India. Each law applies to a different category of citizens.

1. Hindu Succession Act 1956, applicable to Hindu, Sikh, Jain and Buddhist.

2. Indian Succession Act 1925, applicable to Christian, Parsi and Jews.

3. The Muslim Personal Law (Shariat) application Act 1937, applicable to Muslim.

LEGAL STATUS OF NOMINEE

1. A nominee is the custodian (trustee) of the deceased assets. If a nominee is appointed, the deceased's assets go in the hands of a nominee. The entity who handovers the assets of the deceased is legally discharged of the obligation.

2. The Will of the deceased decides that the nominee is the legal heir of the assets or not.

3. There are some exceptions to the above. In the case of company shares, Insurance policies and Employee provident fund, the nominee is the default beneficiary.

COMMON TERMS

1. ESTATE: is the net worth of the person. The sum of a person's assets less liabilities.

2. INTESTATE: A person dies without making a Will.

3. TESTAMENT: Will in written form is called testament.

4. TESTATOR: A person who makes a Will is called Testator.

5. EXECUTOR: a person appointed by the testator for the distribution of assets as per the Will is called an executor.

6. PROBATE: A certificate issued by the court certifying that the Will is valid.

7. CODICIL: Addendum to a Will prepared by the testator. It will become a part of the Will.

Printed in Great Britain
by Amazon

85608593R00029